SMALL LOFTS

PETITS LOFTS

KLEINE LOFTS

SMALL LOFTS
PETITS LOFTS
KLEINE LOFTS

evergreen

EVERGREEN is an imprint of

Taschen GmbH

© 2006 TASCHEN GmbH

Hohenzollernring 53, D-50672 Köln

www.taschen.com

Editor Editrice Redakteur:
Simone Schleifer

English translation Traduction anglaise Englische Übersetzung:
Matthew Clarke

French translation Traduction française Französische Übersetzung:
Marion Westerhoff

German translation Traduction allemande Deutsche Übersetzung:
Susanne Engler

Proofreading Relecture Korrektur lesen:
Caroline Rouquet

Art director Direction artistique Art Direktor:
Mireia Casanovas Soley

Graphic design and layout Mise en page et maquette Graphische Gestaltung und Layout:
Oriol Serra Juncosa

Printed by Imprimé par Gedruckt durch:
Gráficas Toledo, Spain

ISBN-13: 978-3-8228-2785-7
ISBN-10: 3-8228-2785-1

Social and economic events during the 20th century gave rise to new models of life, which in turn created new types of homes reflecting each one of these new disciplines. Post-industrial developments and the spread of information technology reflect diametrically opposed living trends. On the one hand, a legacy of living in old industrial spaces leads to a search for clear, open spaces with generous dimensions in which the domestic duties can be distributed arbitrarily. This trend coined the term loft. On the other hand, the increasing density of the population in city centres has reduced the habitable spaces to minimum dimensions. Together these trends result in the type of home appropriate for current building conditions in large cities. As the title reveals, this book sheds light on these two trends, which, though contradictory, also complement each other.

This selection of projects includes the most diverse residential solutions. The spaces all have reduced proportions and conserve the original architectural characteristics of this type of space employing common strategies such as the conservation of metallic pillars, the elimination of false ceilings, and the restoration of concrete or wooden beams. The new finishes generally respond to the home's practical and functional solutions. The continuity of space, so typical of a loft, resolves the problem of minimal dimensions. The diaphanous quality of the interior is maintained through ethereal, subtle divisions like walls that stop short of the ceiling, sliding doors that disappear, mobile screens that permit changes in the distribution of the residence, or openings and translucent materials that allow light to flow through a divided space.

The projects included here are all under the minimum surface area considered as a loft. Equally useful to architects, designers and city dwellers alike, this book reveals a new way understanding the contemporary interior space.

Les différents événements sociaux et économiques qui ont eu lieu au XXème siècle ont engendré l'apparition de nouveaux modèles de vie qui se sont matérialisés en une typologie très variée d'habitations qui reflètent chacune de ces nouvelles modalités. Les processus post-industriels et l'avancée de la culture de l'information renvoient des tendances d'habitabilité diamétralement opposées. D'une part, et du fait de l'occupation d'anciens espaces industriels, la tendance est à la recherche de superficies diaphanes aux proportions énormes dans lesquelles les différentes pièces peuvent être distribuées de façon arbitraire. Cette tendance a forgé le terme de loft. D'autre part, l'augmentation de la densité de population dans les centres urbains a réduit la superficie habitable à des dimensions minimales. Ces deux courants se juxtaposent pour donner un style d'habitation qui répond aux conditions réelles de construction dans les grandes villes. Le titre évocateur de ce livre fait la lumière sur ces deux tendances, contradictoires mais à la fois complémentaires.

Cette sélection de projets présente les solutions d'habitat les plus diverses. Les espaces, tous de taille réduite, conservent les caractéristiques essentielles de ce type d'espace. Certaines de ces stratégies communes se définissent par le maintien de piliers métalliques, l'élimination de faux plafonds et la restauration des poutres en béton ou en bois. Les nouvelles finitions correspondent en général aux solutions pratiques et fonctionnelles de l'habitat. La fluidité de l'espace, si caractéristique du loft, résout le problème des dimensions minimales. L'aspect diaphane de l'intérieur est le résultat de divisions impalpables et subtiles. Parmi les stratégies innovantes, citons les murs qui n'atteignent pas le plafond ou les murs latéraux, portes coulissantes escamotables, paravents amovibles qui permettent de modifier la distribution de l'espace ou encore fentes et matériaux translucides qui permettent à la lumière de s'infiltrer dans les zones séparées.

Les projets réunis ici présentent tous une surface inférieure à celle répondant à la définition du loft. Ce sont des modèles qui plaisent autant aux architectes et designers qu'aux citadins modernes. Ce livre est un ouvrage outil qui révèle une nouvelle façon d'appréhender l'espace intérieur contemporain.

Soziale sowie wirtschaftliche Ereignisse während des 20. Jahrhunderts ließen neue Lebensmodelle entstehen, die neue Arten von Wohnräumen hervorbrachten, welche ihrerseits diese neuen Tendenzen widerspiegeln. Postindustrielle Entwicklungen und die Ausbreitung der Informationstechnologie verkörpern diese diametral entgegengesetzten Lebenstrends. Einerseits führte der Wunsch danach, in alten industriellen Räumen zu leben, zu einer Suche nach offenen, großdimensionierten Räumen in denen die häuslichen Pflichten flexibel aufgeteilt werden können. Durch diesen Trend entstand das Wohnkonzept Loft. Andererseits führte die stetig ansteigende Bevölkerungsdichte in den Stadtzentren zu einer immer größeren Knappheit an bewohnbarer Fläche. Diese beiden sich gegenüberstehenden Faktoren schafften Wohnkonzepte, die eine Antwort auf die heutzutage vorherrschenden Baubedingungen in großen Städten geben. Wie der Titel dieses Buches bereits ausdrückt, werden in diesem Band Beispiele dieser gegensätzlichen Trends gezeigt, die sich letztendlich jedoch ergänzen.

Wir stellen Ihnen sehr unterschiedliche Wohnungstypen vor, die jedoch gewisse Gemeinsamkeiten haben. Sie sind alle relativ klein und die typischen architektonischen und gestalterischen Merkmale industrieller Räume wurden erhalten. Einige der verwendeten gemeinsamen Strategien waren dabei die Erhaltung der Metallträger, das Entfernen der zweiten Decke und das Freilegen des Betons oder der Holzbalken. Die neuen Oberflächen sind meist sehr praktisch und funktionell. Die Räume sind weiterhin durchgehend, wie es typisch für Lofts ist, wobei dieser durchgängige Raum gleichzeitig das Problem der geringen Größe löst. Sie wirken aufgrund der sehr subtilen, fast flüchtigen Raumteiler weiterhin einheitlich und transparent. Innovative Strategien können Wände sein, die nicht bis zur Decke oder zu Seitenwand reichen, Schiebetüren, die verborgen werden können, mobile Schirme, mit denen man die Anordnung der Wohnung ändern kann, oder Öffnungen sowie durchscheinendes Material, durch das Licht in alle abgetrennten Bereiche fließen kann.

Die Wohnungen, die in diesem Buch vorgestellt werden, liegen alle unter der Mindestgröße, von der man bei einem Loft ausgeht. Sie sind sowohl für Architekten und Innenarchitekten als auch für die Menschen, die in modernen Städten leben, sehr interessant. Dieses Buch kann zu einem Werkzeug werden für diejenigen, die neue Lösungen für zeitgemäße Innenräume suchen.

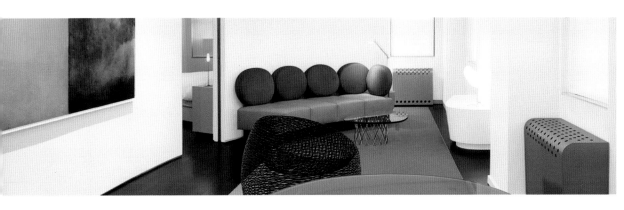

SMALL LOFTS
PETITS LOFTS
KLEINE LOFTS

☐ **Apartment in Milan**

Appartement à Milan

Apartment in Milan

Studio Associato Bettinelli

The floor space here spans a mere 194 square feet, while the height ranges from 36 to 58 feet, making it possible to create two distinct levels. The bathroom is the only space that is closed off; the rest of the house is completely open in order to endow the space with continuity. The first level is occupied by the bathroom, kitchen-dining room, and lounge; the bedroom and closets are situated on the upper level, reached by a steep staircase. The ensemble is painted in several intensities of white, and the variety of shades increases the feeling of spaciousness. The play of light, both natural and artificial, also emphasizes this sensation and contributes to the minimalism of this home. The lighting in this home is simple but effective. The two skylights allow light to penetrate the bedroom and kitchen area, while both the top level and the lounge area have been adorned with small square lamps.

L'habitation occupe une superficie de 18 m² sur une hauteur de 11 et 18 m, ce qui permet la création de deux niveaux différents. La salle de bains est l'unique espace clos, le reste de la demeure étant complètement ouvert pour garder l'espace fluide. Le premier niveau abrite la salle de bains, la cuisine, la salle à manger et la salle de séjour. La chambre à coucher et les armoires se trouvent au premier étage auquel on accède par un escalier assez raide. L'espace est peint en différentes tonalités de blanc et la variété des nuances accentue la sensation de volumes spacieux. De même, les jeux de lumière, tant naturelle qu'artificielle, soulignent cette impression, tout en définissant le style minimaliste de la demeure. L'éclairage est simple, mais optimal : les deux lucarnes de toit permettent à la lumière d'entrer en abondance dans la chambre à coucher et la cuisine. Au rez-de-chaussée et dans la zone du salon, des petites lampes carrées ont été fixées au mur.

Die Wohnung ist 18 m² groß und besitzt eine Höhe zwischen 11 und 18 m, was es ermöglichte, zwei Ebenen zu schaffen. Das Bad ist der einzige geschlossene Bereich, der Rest der Wohnung ist vollständig offen, so dass der Raum fließend wirkt. Auf der ersten Ebene liegen das Bad, die Essküche und das Wohnzimmer, auf der zweiten Ebene das Schlafzimmer und die Schränke. Diese zweite Etage erreicht man über eine steile Treppe. Der Raum wurde in verschiedenen Weißtönen gestrichen, die das Gefühl von Weite verstärken. Ebenso trägt das Spiel mit dem Licht, sowohl Tageslicht als auch künstlichem Licht dazu bei, dass der Raum größer wirkt als er eigentlich ist. Gleichzeitig wird der minimalistische Stil der Wohnung unterstrichen. Die Beleuchtung ist sehr einfach, aber gelungen. Durch zwei Dachfenster fällt viel Tageslicht in das Schlafzimmer und die Küche, und auf der unteren Ebene und im Wohnzimmer wurden kleine quadratische Lampen angebracht.

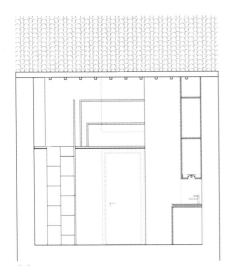

Elevation Élévation Aufriss

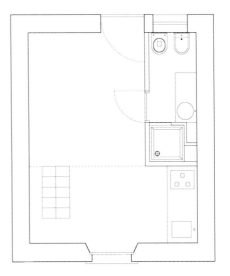

Plan Plan Grundriss

A painstaking assessment of the lighting resulted in the use of white throughout the apartment that is expressed in a range of subtly different tones.

Grâce à une étude minutieuse de l'éclairage, le blanc qui tapisse tout l'appartement se perçoit dans une multitude de nuances.

Die Beleuchtung wurde genau geplant und durchdacht, so dass das Weiß, das in der ganzen Wohnung zu finden ist, in sehr verschiedenen Tönen wahrgenommen wird.

Two skylights flood the interior with natural light.

Grâce aux deux velux, l'intérieur est inondé de lumière naturelle.

Durch zwei Dachfenster erreichte man, dass der gesamte Raum in Tageslicht getaucht wird.

Attic in Zurich
Attique à Zurich
Dachgeschoss in Zürich

Gus Wüstemann

The aim of this project was to create a loft in an old attic that would optimise the magnificent views of the lake, the city and the forest. The first step was to turn the roof into another usable space, and was thus treated as another floor space. The pale walls and ceilings set up a dynamic contrast with the dark beams and furniture. The main characteristic of this project is the hammer-shape structure that has been inserted into the loft to link all the main areas: the office, balcony, bedroom, bathroom, and closets. Instead of creating specific settings, these areas are connected to each other according to their relationship with the hammer. There are no walls in the traditional sense of the term; spaces are defined only by being behind, inside, or next to the inserted structure. The decoration is completed with original furniture, which enhances the personality of this home.

Ce projet est axé sur la conversion d'un ancien grenier qui dispose d'une vue imprenable sur le lac, la ville et la forêt, en loft. La première chose a été de traiter le plafond comme une superficie supplémentaire, de la même manière que le sol. Le contraste entre les tons clairs des murs et des plafonds et les tons sombres des poutres et du mobilier crée un ensemble rayonnant de vitalité. Toutefois, l'originalité de ce projet réside dans une structure en forme de marteau, unissant les pièces principales de l'habitation : bureau, balcon, chambre à coucher, salle de bains et placards. Au lieu de créer des zones différentes, celles-ci sont reliées entre elles en fonction de leur situation sur le marteau. De cette façon, les murs qui ne sont pas conçus traditionnellement, sont situés derrière, à côté ou à l'intérieur du marteau. La décoration affiche un mobilier original qui exalte la personnalité de l'habitation.

Eine alte Dachwohnung, die einen wundervollen Blick auf den See, die Stadt und den Wald bietet, sollte in ein Loft umgebaut werden. Zunächst betrachtete man die Decke als ein weiteres Element, und behandelte sie genauso wie den Fußboden. Der Kontrast zwischen den hellen Tönen der Wände und Decken zu den dunklen Farben der Dachbalken und der Möbel wirkt sehr lebendig. Einzigartig an dieser Planung ist jedoch eine ganz besondere Struktur mit der Form eines Hammers, die die wichtigsten Räume der Wohnung miteinander verbindet, nämlich das Büro, den Balkon, das Schlafzimmer, das Bad und die Schränke. Anstatt verschiedene Bereiche zu schaffen, werden die einzelnen Bereiche mit den anderen je nachdem, wo sie sich in dem Hammer befinden, verbunden. So sind die Wände nicht angeordnet, wie man dies gewohnt ist, sondern sie liegen hinter, im oder neben dem Hammer. Originelle Möbel, die den Charakter der Wohnung unterstreichen, vervollständigen die Dekoration.

... anks to the large windows, the space takes advantage of the magnificent views of the lake, the city, and the forest.

... magnifique paysage qui entoure cette habitation s'invite à l'intérieur grâce à de généreuses baies vitrées.

... e wundervolle Landschaft, die diese Wohnung umgibt, dringt durch riesige Fenster ins Innere.

The pale walls and ceilings set up a dynamic contrast with the dark beams and furniture.

Le contraste entre les tons clairs des murs et des plafonds et les tons sombres des poutres et du mobilier crée un ensemble rayonnant de vitalité.

Der Kontrast zwischen den hellen Farben der Decken und Wände zu den dunklen Holzbalken und Möbeln lässt das Loft sehr lebendig wirken.

☐ Fasan Dwelling
Habitation Fasan
Fasan Wohnung

Johannes Will

Reducing a dwelling to its essential functions can result in a space in which the features are characterized by the space itself and the varying effects of light and shadow. This loft is characterized by its open, fluid space that brings together the basic elements of the residence. The linear aspect was achieved by removing walls and openings and creating subtle and uncluttered circulation areas. One of the most notable elements is the structural partition that divides the dining area from the studio, which adopts a precise design thanks to a careful choice of quality materials such as glass, metal and wood panels. The combination of all these elements generates a highly individualized interior.

Réduire l'habitation à ses fonctions essentielles peut engendrer des espaces dont les effets, par le jeu d'ombres et de lumières, résultent de l'espace même. Le vide, la fluidité spatiale et la concentration d'éléments de base caractérisent ce loft. Pour obtenir cette pureté des lignes, les cloisons et les ouvertures ont été supprimées afin de créer des zones de passage subtiles et légères. Un des points de mire est la cloison sculpturale qui sépare le séjour salle à manger du bureau. La précision du design résulte d'une planification méticuleuse et de matériaux de grande qualité, comme le verre, le métal et le bois. Le mélange de ces éléments définit un intérieur à la fois personnel et original.

Wenn man eine Wohnung auf die grundlegenden Funktionen reduziert, kann ein Raum entstehen, dessen Wirkung auf dem Raum selbst beruht, eine Wirkung, die von dem Spiel mit Licht und Schatten hervorgerufen wird. Der Charakter dieses Lofts wird von der Leere, der räumlichen Kontinuität und der Konzentration der grundlegenden Elemente der Wohnung definiert. Um diese klaren Linien zu erreichen, riss man Wände nieder, schuf Öffnungen und subtile, kaum wahrnehmbare Durchgangsbereiche. Die präzise Gestaltung ist Ergebnis einer sorgfältigen Planung und der Verwendung hochwertiger Materialien wie Glas, Metall und Holz. Dank der Kombination dieser Elemente entstand eine Wohnumgebung mit einer eigenen Ausdrucksweise.

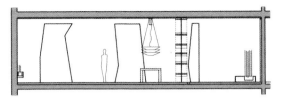

Section Section Schnitt

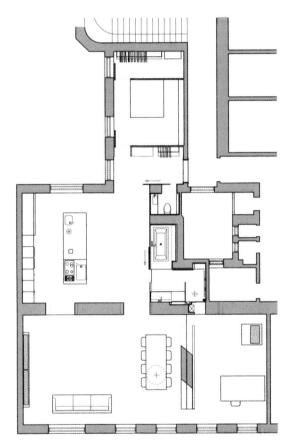

Plan Plan Grundriss

The consistency of the light and the warmth of the wood create a minimalist, yet hospitable environment.

La douceur et l'emplacement de l'éclairage, ainsi que la qualité du bois, créent une atmosphère minimaliste et accueillante à la fois.

Sanfte Lichtquellen am richtigen Platz sowie edles Holz lassen eine minimalistische, aber gleichzeitig einladende Atmosphäre entstehen.

To achieve the esthetic harmony that pervades this loft, all kitchen appliances are concealed behind handle-free sliding panels.

Tout l'électroménager de la cuisine disparaît derrière des panneaux coulissants sans poignées pour conserver l'harmonie qui caractérise ce loft élégant.

Alle Haushaltsgeräte in der Küche sind hinter gleitenden Paneelen ohne Griffe versteckt, um so die Harmonie, die im gesamten Loft herrscht, nicht zu stören.

]
e combination of colors, the texture of the wood, and the purity of the lines result in a bathroom that is austere and elegant.

mélange de couleurs, la texture du bois et la pureté des lignes forment une salle de bains tout en sobriété et élégance.

Kombination der Farben, der Textur des Holzes und der reinen Linien schafft ein schlichtes und elegantes Badezimmer.

☐ Apartment in New York
Appartement à New-York
Apartment in New York

Morris Sato Studio

This apartment is a superb illustration of how a small space can be turned into an spacious personal refuge. The conversion revolves around a curved wall that completely transforms the rectangular perimeter of the original space, creating a feeling of movement and expansiveness. As no good views were on offer, the windows were adorned with screens that filter the light and extend the spotless white of the walls. Floors of various colors and materials combine with specially designed furniture to form an interior landscape of cool, elegant colors. The main space is dominated by an acrylic table with a base of metal rods tipped with LED lights that cover the ceiling with swathes of metallic blue. One of the most interesting features of the project is undoubtedly the ceiling, as it leaves the structure of the building partially exposed, as if it were an urban archeological relic.

Cet appartement est un magnifique exemple de conversion d'un petit espace en un vaste refuge empreint de personnalité. L'axe principal de la restauration tourne autour d'un mur tout en courbe qui transforme complètement le périmètre rectangulaire de l'espace initial, générant une sensation de mouvement et d'espace. Suite à l'absence de vue intéressante, les fenêtres ont été dotées d'écrans qui tamisent la lumière, préservant la continuité de la blancheur immaculée des murs. Carrelages de différentes couleurs et matériaux différents conjugués aux meubles de design unique, esquissent un paysage intérieur aux tons froids et élégants. Point de mire de l'espace principal, une table en acrylique, avec un pied constitué de baguettes métalliques et des extrémités en LED dont le reflet baigne le plafond d'une couleur bleu métallique. De toute évidence, le plafond est une des réalisations les plus remarquables du projet : la structure de l'édifice est partiellement apparente, à l'instar de vestiges archéologiques urbains.

Diese Wohnung ist ein wundervolles Beispiel dafür, wie man einen kleinen Raum in eine weite und persönliche Wohnumgebung verwandeln kann. Die Hauptachse des Eingriffs ist eine gekrümmte Mauer, die den rechteckigen Grundriss des Raumes völlig verändert und ein Gefühl von Bewegung und Weite entstehen lässt. Da es keine schöne Aussicht gab, wurden die Fenster mit Schirmen geschlossen, durch die sich das Licht filtert und die das makellose Weiß der Wände fortsetzen. Der Bodenbelag in verschiedenen Farben und aus verschiedenen Materialien und die selbst entworfenen Möbel schaffen eine innere Landschaft in kalten und eleganten Tönen. Im Hauptraum fällt ein Acryltisch auf, der einen Unterbau aus Metallstäben hat, die in Leds enden, deren Reflexe die Decke in ein metallisches Blau tauchen. Eines der interessanten Elemente ist eben diese Decke, die teilweise die Struktur des Gebäudes sichtbar lässt, als ob es sich um urbane archäologische Fundstellen handeln würde.

Floors in various colors and materials combine with specially designed furniture to create an interior landscape with cold but elegant tones.

Carrelages de différentes couleurs et matériaux divers conjugués aux meubles de design original, façonnent un paysage intérieur aux tons froids et élégants

Der Bodenbelag in verschiedenen Farben und aus verschiedenen Materialien und die selbst entworfenen Möbel schaffen eine innere Landschaft in eleganten Tönen.

Loft in São Paulo
Loft à São Paulo
Loft in São Paulo

Brunete Fraccaroli

The architect Brunete Fraccaroli had no problems in the remodeling of this attractive space, which is bursting with color and freshness. It was agreed that the old structure of columns and iron beams would be maintained, with the simple addition of a mezzanine, where the filmmaker's office and master bedroom could be located. The day area fills the lower floor, housing the kitchen, the main living room, and a small room furnished with a music system and flat-screen television. The original brick walls have been preserved, which provide warmth, and contrast with the tempered-glass sheet panels. The transparency of this material blends with the original architecture and emphasizes the complementary nature of the modifications, as well as showering the loft with light.

L'architecte Brunete Fraccaroli a été chargée de remodeler ce bel espace pétillant de couleur et de fraîcheur. L'ancienne structure conservée — colonnes et poutres d'acier — ne s'est vue ajouter qu'un entresol pour accueillir le bureau et la chambre à coucher du propriétaire. L'étage inférieur héberge la zone de jour avec la cuisine, le séjour principal et un petit espace réservé à l'équipement audiovisuel et la télévision. Les murs ont gardé les briques d'origine qui rendent l'intérieur chaleureux et contrastent avec les panneaux de verre laminé et trempé. La transparence de cette matière évite d'entraver l'architecture initiale et les modifications deviennent alors complémentaires. La luminosité intérieure et le modernisme du mobilier sont les deux caractéristiques essentielles de ce loft.

Die Architektin Brunete Fraccaroli erhielt den Auftrag, diesen schönen Raum voller Farbe und Frische umzugestalten. Die Originalstruktur mit den Säulen und Eisenträgern blieb erhalten. Man fügte nur ein Zwischengeschoss ein, auf dem sich das Büro der Eigentümerin und das große Schlafzimmer befinden. Auf der unteren Etage liegen die Räume, die man tagsüber benutzt, also die Küche, das Wohnzimmer und ein kleiner Medienbereich mit Stereoanlage und Fernseher. An den Wänden ließ man die Originalziegel den Blicken frei, wodurch die Wohnung freundlich wirkt, gleichzeitig aber auch ein Kontrast zu den Paneelen aus gewalztem Hartglas entstehen lässt. Die Transparenz dieses Materials machte es möglich, die Originalarchitektur zu erhalten und nur Änderungen vorzunehmen, die als Ergänzung dienen. Die Helligkeit in den Räumen und die modernen Möbel sind die Elemente, die in diesem Loft besonders auffallen.

...he use of tempered glass creates visual continuity between the levels.

...e verre trempé, matériau utilisé pour la construction de l'entresol, favorise la continuité visuelle entre les niveaux.

...as Zwischengeschoss wurde aus Hartglas konstruiert, so dass eine visuelle Kontinuität zwischen den Ebenen entsteht .

Old and new efforttessly coexist in this interior, resulting in an industrial, yet warm and hospitable dwelling.

Le nouveau et l'ancien se marient et se mêlent avec une surprenante facilité dans un intérieur aux réminiscences industrielles, au demeurant très accueillant.

Alt und neu vermischen sich und werden in diesen Räumen, die an die industrielle Vergangenheit erinnern, problemlos miteinander kombiniert.

original brick walls contrast well with the tempered-glass-sheet panels applied in the shed.

rique d'origine des murs crée un contraste marqué avec le verre laminé des combles.

Originalziegel der Wände bilden einen starken Kontrast zu dem gewalzten Glas der oberen Ebene.

Loft in New York
Loft à New-York
Loft in New York

Choon Choi Design

The architects of this small loft in New York have managed to fit together various volumes to achieve a tight-fitting jigsaw that takes full advantage of the space. The different levels of the platform combine with the walkway to create sufficient space for two bedrooms, closets, and a bathroom area. A metal staircase is situated between the two bedrooms on the platform. Its metal finish adds a contemporary, industrial touch that recalls the staircases found on ships. The range of colors is deliberately restricted by the choice of materials: wood for the horizontal surfaces and white for the walls. The kitchen is set underneath the platform, and the bedroom module is separated from the living area by glass, allowing natural light to enter. In this loft, the use of space has been calculated down to the last centimeter; the result is an expansive home flooded with light, where one space flows into the next.

Les architectes de ce petit loft new-yorkais ont pu assembler divers volumes pour obtenir un puzzle parfaitement ajusté qui maximalise l'espace. Les différents niveaux de la plate-forme agrémentée d'une passerelle, créent un espace assez généreux pour accueillir deux chambres, plusieurs placards et une salle de bains. Un escalier métallique, situé entre les deux chambres à coucher de la plate-forme, donne à l'habitation un caractère contemporain et industriel, et n'est pas sans rappeler l'échelle d'un navire. Les matériaux employés déclinent une palette de couleurs volontairement limitée : bois pour les surfaces horizontales et blanc pour les verticales, comme pour les murs. La cuisine se trouve sous la plate-forme et la zone des chambres est séparée du séjour par une vitre qui laisse passer la lumière naturelle. L'étude minutieuse de l'espace permet de l'optimiser au millimètre près. Il en résulte une habitation ample et lumineuse où les espaces sont fluides.

Die Architekten, die dieses kleine Loft in New York planten, wussten, wie man verschiedene Volumen so miteinander verbindet, dass ein gelungenes Puzzle entsteht, das den vorhandenen Raum maximal nutzt. Die verschiedenen Ebenen der Plattform und ein Laufsteg ließen genug Platz entstehen, um zwei Zimmer, verschiedene Schränke und ein Bad zu schaffen. Eine Metalltreppe zwischen den beiden Schlafzimmern auf der Plattform, die an eine Schiffstreppe erinnert, lässt die Wohnung modern und industriell wirken. Die verwendeten Materialien schränken mit Absicht die Farbpalette ein. An den horizontalen Flächen findet man Holz und die vertikalen Flächen wie die Wände sind weiß. Die Küche liegt unter der Plattform und die Schlafzimmer sind vom Wohnzimmer durch eine Glaswand getrennt, durch die Tageslicht fällt. Jeder Millimeter des Raumes wurde ausgenutzt, so dass eine weite und helle Wohnung mit fließenden Räumen entstand.

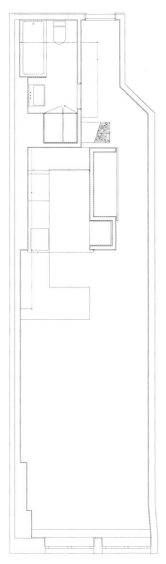

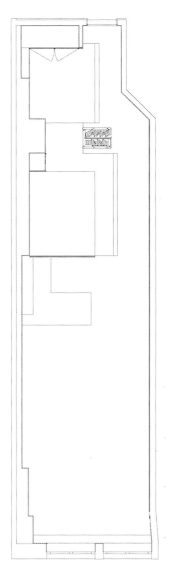

Ground floor Rez-de-chaussée Erdgeschoss   First floor Premier étage Erstes Obergeschoss

The range of colors is deliberately restricted by the choice of materials: wood for the horizontal surfaces and white for the vertical surfaces.

Les matériaux employés déclinent une palette de couleurs limitée : bois pour les surfaces horizontales et blanc pour les verticales.

Durch die benutzten Materialien wurde die Farbpalette bewusst eingeschränkt, die waagerechten Flächen sind aus Holz und die senkrechten Wände weiß.

The metal finish of the staircase adds a contemporary, industrial touch that recalls the interior of a ship.

La finition en métal de l'escalier lui confère un aspect à la fois contemporain et industriel, évoquant l'intérieur d'un navire.

Die metallische Farbe der Treppe lässt den Raum modern und industriell wirken, und erinnert gleichzeitig an Schiffstreppen.

Locher Apartment
Appartement Locher
Locher Apartment

Spoerri Thommen Architekten

The building in which this apartment is set dates from the 1970s and is located in an industrial neighbourhood. The anonymous exterior contrasts with the owner,s desire for a unique interior. The aim of the refurbishment was to transform a standard four-bedroom apartment into a spacious loft, which was made possible given the ideal conditions: abundant light and a structure that enabled the removal of partitions and walls. The apartment had to include all the required services while giving priority to a relaxation area and an organic visual approach. The most eye-catching features of this home include a large, upholstered wall that hides the kitchen and bathroom, and an elegant bathtub that serves as the central dividing element and a symbol of relaxation. The soft colour scheme and minimal decoration imbue the apartment with the desired atmosphere of relaxation and tranquillity.

L'édifice qui abrite cet appartement est une construction des années soixante dix, située dans un quartier industriel. Le caractère anonyme de l'extérieur contraste avec le besoin d'individualisme de la propriétaire. La restauration vise à convertir un appartement de quatre chambres en un ample loft, l'habitation réunissant les conditions idéales pour ce faire, à savoir, la possibilité d'éliminer les murs et l'abondance de lumière. L'appartement devait intégrer tous les services nécessaires, en donnant la priorité à une zone de relaxation et à une esthétique organique. Un grand mur revêtu d'un papier peint qui masque la cuisine et la salle de bains et une élégante baignoire servant d'élément séparateur central et symbole de repos, sont un des points de mire caractéristiques de cette habitation. Douceur des tons et décoration minimale confèrent à l'ensemble l'atmosphère de relaxation et de calme recherchée.

Das Gebäude, in dem sich diese Wohnung befindet, stammt aus den Siebzigerjahren und liegt in einem Industrieviertel. Der anonyme Charakter des Viertels steht im Gegensatz zu dem Wunsch nach Individualität, den die Wohnungseigentümerin hegte. Der Umbau dieser Vierzimmerwohnung zu einem Loft war möglich, weil die Wohnung die idealen Voraussetzungen für einen solchen Umbau aufwies. Die Struktur machte es möglich, Wände zu entfernen, und reichlich Tageslicht einfallen zu lassen. Es sollten alle notwendigen Räume und Wohnfunktionen enthalten sein, aber besonders wichtig war es, einen Bereich der Ruhe und organischer Ästhetik zu schaffen. Ein besonders auffallendes Element in dieser Wohnung ist die große, tapezierte Wand, hinter der sich die Küche und das Bad mit der eleganten Badewanne befinden. Sie ist das zentrale teilende Element und ein Symbol für Ruhe. Die zarten Farben und die zurückhaltende Dekoration schaffen die entspannende und ruhige Atmosphäre in der Wohnung, die sich die Kundin wünschte.

The loft required a conventional domestic program, but the client wanted it to have an organic look and a relaxation area.

L'appartement devait suivre une esthétique organique et avoir une zone de relaxation.

In dem Loft sollte man die üblichen Wohnfunktionen finden, aber gleichzeitig wünschte sich der Kunde eine organische Ästhetik und einen Bereich zum Entspannen.

The soft color scheme and minimal decoration imbue the apartment with the desired atmosphere of relaxation and tranquility.

La douceur des tons et la décoration minimaliste confèrent à l'appartement l'atmosphère relaxante et apaisante recherchée.

Die zarten Farbe und die minimalistische Dekoration schaffen die entspannende und ruhige Atmosphäre in der Wohnung, die man sich wünschte.

Loft in Bergamo
Loft à Bergamo
Loft in Bergamo

Studio Associato Bettinelli

An urban and contemporary ambience emanates from this loft characterized by simplicity of décor and high-quality finishes. The living room, which boasts a polished cement floor, is situated between two levels articulated around an elegant staircase that constitutes the centerpiece of this loft. The décor is reduced to the basics, featuring a sofa and television flanked by a row of books along the floor that lead to an open-plan bedroom. The light that flows into the bedroom is filtered by roller blinds made from lightweight fabric. The upper level of this loft houses the dining room and kitchen area, which is transformed by the placement of furniture and freestanding appliances into a flexible and dynamic space.

Une ambiance citadine et contemporaine émane de ce loft qui affiche une simplicité de décoration et des finitions de grande qualité. Le salon dont le revêtement est en ciment poli, est situé entre deux niveaux, et s'articule autour d'un escalier tout en élégance, élément central du loft. La décoration est réduite au minimum : un divan et une télévision, entourés de livres disposés à même le sol, forment un élément visuel intéressant qui mène, à l'instar d'un guide, à une simple chambre à coucher sans aucune cloison pour la séparer de cet univers. La lumière qui la pénètre est tamisée par le tissu léger des rideaux. Le niveau supérieur du loft abrite la cuisine et la salle à manger, qui se transforment en espaces flexibles et dynamiques grâce à la disposition du mobilier et des appareils électroménagers.

Ein urbanes und modernes Ambiente geht von diesem Loft aus, das durch seine schlichte Ausstattung und die qualitativ hochwertige Verkleidung gekennzeichet ist. Das Wohnzimmer mit dem Fußboden aus poliertem Beton befindet sich zwischen zwei Ebenen und umgibt eine elegante Treppe, die das zentrale Element dieses Lofts darstellt. Die Ausstattung wurde auf ein Minimum reduziert; ein Sofa und ein Fernseher umgeben von Büchern auf dem Fußboden bilden ein visuell sehr anziehendes Element, das gleichzeitig zu dem einfachen Schlafzimmer führt, für das es kein anderes trennendes Element gibt. Das Licht fällt durch Gardinen aus luftigem Stoff ins Schlafzimmer. Auf der obersten Ebene des Lofts befinden sich die Küche und das Esszimmer, die aufgrund der Anordnung der Möbel und der unabhängigen Haushaltsgeräte sehr flexibel und dynamisch sind.

The dining room table is positioned next to the kitchen. The design of the loft creates a functional and elegant space.

La table de la salle à manger se trouve près de la cuisine : cette continuité du design crée un espace à la fois fonctionnel et élégant.

Der Esstisch steht in der Nähe der Küche, so entsteht durch die Kontinuität der Gestaltung ein funktioneller, aber gleichzeitig eleganter Raum.

light that flows into the bedroom is filtered by translucent screens.

umière qui traverse la chambre à coucher est tamisée grâce à des stores réalisés en tissu léger.

s Licht fällt durch Gardinen aus luftigem Stoff ins Schlafzimmer.

Duplex in Born
Duplex dans le Born
Duplex im Born

Joan Pons Forment

This elegant and modern one-bedroom duplex loft is located in one of the most cosmopolitan and fashionable areas of the city. The hall, kitchen, living room, and dining room come together in a single space on the lower level, with the bathroom and master bedroom on the upper floor. The black-and-white color scheme is broken by the presence of grays and the occasional touch of red. The living room is furnished with a comfortable sofa and a white fur rug that provide an interesting contrast against the black wall at the other end of the room. The kitchen, which combines white with steel, fits perfectly with the simplicity of the space, owing to its refined lines. On the upper floor, the studio and bedroom flow into one another and have been designed in harmony with the rest of the loft, employing simple lines and elegant furniture.

Ce duplex, à la fois élégant et moderne, doté d'une chambre à coucher, est situé dans une des zones les plus branchées de la ville. Le couloir, la cuisine, le salon et la salle à manger se partagent un espace unique à l'étage inférieur, la salle de bains et la chambre à coucher principale étant à l'étage supérieur. La gamme de noir et blanc est interrompue par la présence de nuances grises et d'une touche occasionnelle de rouge. Le salon est meublé d'un divan confortable et d'un tapis en peau blanche, offrant un contraste intéressant avec le mur noir situé à l'autre extrémité de la pièce à vivre. La cuisine, dans son alliance de blanc et d'acier, et forte de la finesse de ses lignes, s'intègre à merveille dans cet espace tout en sobriété. A l'étage supérieur, le studio côtoie la chambre à coucher, dont le design s'harmonise au reste du loft par la simplicité de ses lignes et au mobilier sombre mais élégant.

Diese elegante und moderne Maisonette mit einem Schlafzimmer, liegt in einer der modernsten Zonen der Stadt. Der Flur, die Küche, das Wohnzimmer und das Esszimmer sind in einem einzigen Raum auf der unteren Ebene untergebracht; das Bad und das Schlafzimmer liegen auf der oberen Ebene. Das schwarzweiße Farbschema wird durch Grautöne und kleine Nuancen in Rot unterbrochen. Das Wohnzimmer ist mit einem bequemen Sofa und einem Teppich aus weißem Fell ausgestattet, die einen interessanten Kontrast zu der schwarzen Wand auf der anderen Seite des Raumes bilden. In der Küche wurde die Farbe Weiß mit Stahl kombiniert, eine ausgezeichnete Wahl, um den einfachen Raum mit seinen edlen Linien zu gestalten. Auf der oberen Ebene verbindet sich das Arbeitszimmer mit dem Schlafzimmer, beide in den gleichen, einfachen Linien gestaltet und mit schlichten, aber eleganten Möbeln ausgestattet, so dass ein harmonisches Gesamtbild entsteht.

]
e graceful, lightweight staircase takes on a sculptural feel and contrasts with the white and dark gray color scheme.

scalier, tout en légèreté et élégance, prend des allures sculpturales qui contrastent avec la palette de touches de couleurs déclinant blanc, noir et nuances grises.

e hübsche, leichte Treppe bildet einen Kontrast zu den Weiß- und Dunkelgrautönen und wirkt fast wie eine Skulptur.

The kitchen, which combines white with steel, fits perfectly with the simplicity of the space, owing to its refined lines.

La cuisine, dans son alliance de blanc et d'acier et forte de la finesse de ses lignes, s'intègre à merveille dans cet espace tout en sobriété.

In der Küche wurde die Farbe Weiß mit Stahl kombiniert, eine ausgezeichnete Wahl, um den einfachen Raum mit seinen edlen Linien zu gestalten.

minimalist design of this loft creates an atmosphere that transmits tranquility. The natural light accentuates this effect and can be used imaginatively.

design minimaliste crée une atmosphère sereine : la lumière naturelle, utilisée avec imagination, exalte cet effet.

minimalistische Gestaltung schafft eine gelassene Atmosphäre, und das Tageslicht, das mit viel Phantasie eingesetzt wurde, unterstreicht diese Wirkung.

☐ Apartment in Brussels
Appartement à Bruxelles
Apartment in Brüssel

Popoff-Bouquelle

The design of this loft was reduced to a simple structural expression. Distributed around a courtyard, the interior areas and bedrooms are articulated around this central space. The columns and materials like cement and concrete lend the apartment the industrial aesthetic desired by the owners. Expansive glass walls provide abundant natural light, while a series of folding closets are situated throughout the loft to define or conceal different areas such as the kitchen, which is disguised by one of the units. Along this wall, the same system integrates a library and studio. These elements establish an effective way of defining space and creating different atmospheres. Bright and vivid colours were used to imbue the loft with warmth and vitality.

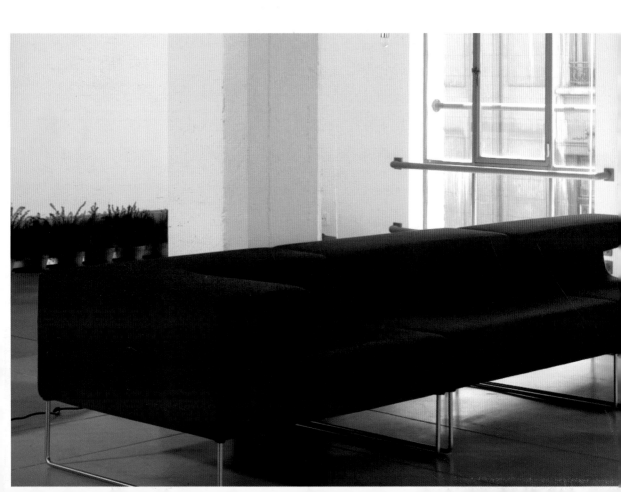

Ce loft a été réalisé en réduisant la construction à sa simple expression structurelle. Le plan évolue autour d'un patio intérieur et définit la distribution des pièces en fonction de cet espace central. Les colonnes et les matériaux, à l'instar du ciment et du béton confèrent à l'appartement une esthétique industrielle, effet spécialement recherché par les propriétaires. La grande superficie vitrée des murs dispense une abondante lumière naturelle. Une série de placards aux portes en accordéon est répartie dans tout le loft. Ces éléments permettent de définir, mettre en valeur ou masquer les différentes pièces, comme la cuisine, qui disparaît derrière certaines de ces unités. Sur un même mur, et selon le même système, on trouve la bibliothèque et le bureau. Ces éléments instaurent un jeu qui permet de délimiter un espace et de créer différents univers. Les couleurs vives et brillantes qu'affiche l'intérieur, créent un agencement rempli de vitalité et de chaleur.

Dieses Loft ist das Ergebnis der Reduktion einer Konstruktion auf einen einfachen strukturellen Ausdruck. Die Räume umgeben einen Innenhof, der das Zentrum bildet, von dem die einzelnen Bereiche abgehen. Die Säulen und Materialien wie Zement und Beton schaffen in der Wohnung eine industrielle Ästhetik, wie dies auch ausdrücklicher Wunsch der Eigentümer war. Durch große verglaste Flächen in den Wänden fällt viel Tageslicht ein. Im ganzen Loft befinden sich Schränke mit Falttüren, die die verschiedenen Räume definieren, zeigen oder verbergen, so zum Beispiel die Küche, die sich hinter einem dieser Möbel befindet. An der gleichen Wand liegen die Bibliothek und das Büro, die mit dem gleichen System abgetrennt oder geöffnet werden. So ist es möglich, auf fast spielerische Weise einen Bereich einzugrenzen und verschiedene Umgebungen zu schaffen. Die starken und glänzenden Farben lassen den Raum warm und lebendig wirken.

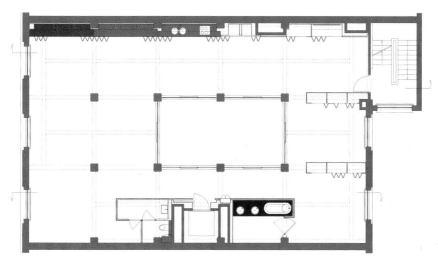

Plan Plan Grundriss

Bright, shiny colors combine to bring vitality and warmth to this otherwise rather cold space.

Les couleurs vives et brillantes qu'affiche l'intérieur, créent un agencement dynamique et chaleureux.

Die starken und glänzenden Farben lassen den Raum warm und lebendig wirken.

The windows are built into glass walls, maximizing the flow of light into the apartment.

La grande superficie vitrée des murs dispense une abondante lumière naturelle.

Durch große verglaste Flächen in den Wänden fällt viel Tageslicht ein.

Miami Beach Pied-à-Terre
Résidence à Miami Beach
Wohnung in Miami Beach

Pablo Uribe – Studio Uribe

This small loft was designed for a couple living in Miami Beach as a second residence with easy access to the beach and in which to take a quick shower and host informal gatherings and dinner parties. Because of the sporadic use of the apartment, the project was simplified so that all household functions could be integrated into a single space. The existing interior walls were eliminated to gain space. The polished cement floor and aluminium windows bring simplicity and elegance to the interior, drawing inspiration from the building itself, which was constructed in 1967. The kitchen is situated inside the entrance hall next to the dining area and leads into the living room. The bedroom and bathroom are situated adjacent to a small studio. Positioning the bed opposite the sofa creates a sensation of amplitude and continuity throughout the space.

Ce petit loft a été conçu pour un couple qui possède déjà une maison à Miami Beach. Mais cette demeure n'étant pas située au bord de la mer, les propriétaires ont souhaité avoir une résidence secondaire sur le front de mer pour passer la journée à la plage, prendre une douche et organiser un dîner informel. Le cahier des charges était simple : l'utilisation sporadique de cette habitation permettait d'intégrer les fonctions dans un espace unique. L'édifice de 1967 hébergeant le loft, a défini l'esthétique du design intérieur. Les murs existants ont été éliminés pour gagner de l'espace utile. Le ciment poli utilisé pour le sol et l'aluminium des fenêtres, engendrent un intérieur simple et élégant. La cuisine se trouve à l'entrée, à côté du séjour salle à manger. La chambre à coucher et la salle de bains se trouvent sur la droite du petit bureau. La disposition face à face du lit et du divan crée une impression de largesse et de continuité de l'espace.

Dieses kleine Loft wurde für ein Paar entworfen, das bereits ein Haus in Miami Beach besitzt. Die Eigentümer wünschten sich eine Zweitwohnung am Meer, in der sie einen Tag am Strand genießen, duschen oder ein lockeres Abendessen im Freundeskreis organisieren können. Ein einfacher Auftrag. Da es sich um eine Wohnung handelt, die nur manchmal benutzt wird, konnten alle Wohnfunktionen in einem einzigen Raum untergebracht werden. Das Gebäude, in dem sich dieses Loft befindet, ist aus dem Jahr 1967, und die Architekten ließen sich von der Ästhetik jener Zeit inspirieren. Existierende Wände wurden niedergerissen, um Nutzfläche zu gewinnen. Die Böden sind aus poliertem Beton und die Fenster aus Aluminium, so dass das Gesamtbild einfach, aber elegant wirkt. Die Küche liegt am Eingang, direkt am kombinierten Wohn- und Esszimmer. Das Schlafzimmer und das Bad befinden sich auf der rechten Seite der kleinen Studiowohnung. Durch die Anordnung des Bettes vor dem Sofa entsteht ein Gefühl von Weite und Kontinuität im Raum.

e polished cement floor and aluminum windows bring simplicity and elegance to the interior.

ciment poli du sol et l'aluminium des fenêtres engendrent un intérieur sobre et élégant.

e Aluminiumfenster und der Boden aus poliertem Beton schaffen eine einfache, jedoch elegante Wohnumgebung.

The use of light tones creates a refreshing atmosphere enhanced by the colors of the interior furnishings.

Les couleurs claires engendrent une atmosphère chaleureuse. Les touches de couleur de certains meubles ajoutent fraîcheur et vitalité à cet intérieur.

Die hellen Farben erzeugen eine warme Atmosphäre, und einige Möbelstücke in kräftigen Farben lassen den Raum frisch und lebendig wirken.

Pink House
Maison Pink
Pink Haus

Filippo Bombace

The old nineteen-fifties building that accommodates this apartment strikes the note for this design, wich emphasizes the original structure while providing it with a refreshed, modern appearance. The apartment layout is derived from a rather irregular geometric plan that influences our perception of the interior space. The proposed solution maintains a balance between the original structure, the available budget and the clients' requirements. Instead of maintaining to the intricacies of the original interior plan, which would have resulted in very extravagant effects, a simpler approach was taken by highlighting the 43-foot corridor and stressing the role of the living room through the use of a variety of ceiling heights. Translucent curtains help to define different areas, and the nature and arrangement of the furniture make allusions to the former character of the residence.

L'ancien édifice des années cinquante, qui abrite cet appartement, est à l'origine de ce projet qui exalte la structure originale de l'édifice tout en imprégnant la demeure de modernité et de dynamisme. La planimétrie de l'appartement se base sur une géométrie plutôt irrégulière qui influe sur la perception de l'espace intérieur. Le projet maintient l'équilibre entre la structure initiale, les contraintes budgétaires et les souhaits du client. Face à la géométrie complexe de l'appartement – qui aurait généré des formes extravagantes –, l'architecte a trouvé une solution simple qui permet de rehausser le couloir de presque 13 m et d'accentuer le rôle du séjour grâce aux différentes hauteurs du faux plafond. La transparence des rideaux définit les pièces à vivre, tandis que les formes et la disposition du mobilier rappellent la distribution initiale de l'appartement.

Ausgangspunkt bei der Planung dieser Wohnung war ein altes Gebäude aus den Fünfzigerjahren. Die Originalstruktur sollte betont werden, gleichzeitig sollte die Wohnung jedoch modern und dynamisch wirken. Der Grundriss ist ziemlich unregelmäßig, was die Wahrnehmung des Raumes stark beeinflusst. Die Planer wussten es, ein Gleichgewicht zwischen der Originalstruktur, den zur Verfügung stehenden Mitteln und den Anforderungen der Kunden zu schaffen. Auf Grund der verwinkelten Struktur der Wohnung, durch die sehr extravagante Formen entstanden wären, fand man eine einfache Lösung, die darin bestand, den fast 13 m langen Flur zu betonen und im Wohnzimmern mit verschiedenen Höhen der eingezogenen, falschen Decke zu arbeiten. Die Räume werden durch transparente Gardinen definiert, während die Formen und die Anordnung der Möbel auf die Originalaufteilung der Wohnung anspielen.

Translucent curtains help to define different areas and to structure the space.

Les transparences issues des rideaux contribuent à définir les sphères de vie et à structurer l'espace.

Die transparenten Gardinen sind Elemente, die die Räume mit definieren und strukturieren.

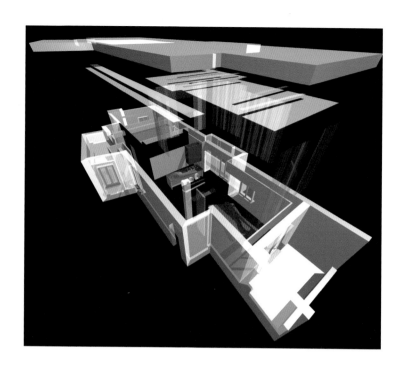

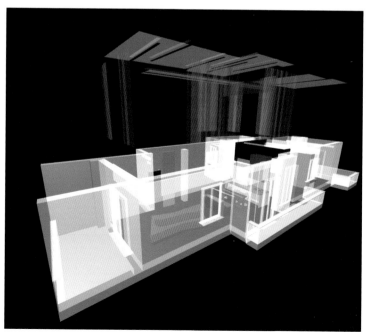

Exploded views Vues éclatées Einzelteildarstellungen

The architect has described this project as 'a dance of luminous lines of colour underlining the ambiguous geometry within the dwelling'.

Pour l'architecte, ce projet est à l'image d'une danse de lignes lumineuses colorées qui mettent en relief les lignes géométriques floues de l'habitation.

Der Architekt definiert diese Wohnung als einen Tanz leuchtender farbiger Linien, die die gegensätzliche Geometrie der Räumlichkeiten unterstreicht.

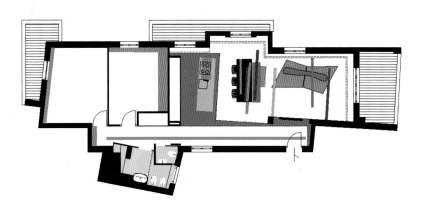

Plan Plan Grundriss

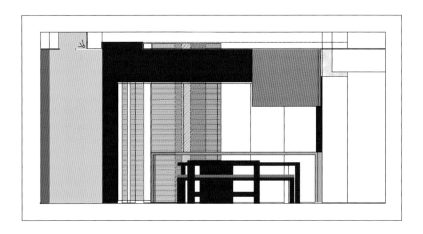

Section Section Schnitt

Wasch Residence
Résidence Wasch
Wasch Residenz

Alden Maddry

This building was formerly a hotel and more recently a photographic studio, before being acquired by the present owners. The distribution of the entire space was redesigned, and walls and separations were eliminated to transform it into an apartment. The dining room and kitchen lead into the living room, where a quick breakfast or informal meal can be enjoyed at a small bar. Translucent sliding panels with resin detailing give the loft a dynamic quality, revealing a second living room that amplifies the apartment and can also be used as an intimate guest bedroom. The principal aim was to maximize the amount of light, hence the use of pivoting clerestory windows, which improve the air circulation and take full advantage of the ceiling height.

Avant son acquisition par les propriétaires actuels, cet édifice a été tour à tour un hôtel puis un studio de photographes. Pour le transformer définitivement en habitation, les partitions ont été éliminées, entraînant une redistribution de l'espace. Les pièces les plus intéressantes sont la salle à manger et la cuisine, ouverte sur le salon où un petit bar permet de prendre un petit déjeuner rapide ou un dîner informel. Des panneaux coulissants et translucides, en partie constitués de résine, imprègnent le loft de dynamisme. Ils s'ouvrent sur un deuxième salon, ce qui contribue à agrandir l'appartement. Une fois fermés, l'espace redevient intime et se métamorphose en chambre d'amis. L'idée directrice de cette restauration est d'obtenir un maximum de lumière naturelle dans toutes les pièces. À cet effet, les fenêtres horizontales se nichent dans la partie supérieure des murs, une vitre pivotante permettant de ventiler le loft.

Bevor dieses Gebäude von den heutigen Eigentümern erworben wurde, war es ein Hotel und später ein Fotografiestudio. Für den definitiven Umbau in eine Wohnung wurden Wände abgerissen und die Aufteilung neu geplant. Die auffallendsten Räume sind das Esszimmer und die Küche, die sich zum Wohnzimmer öffnen. Hier befindet sich ein kleiner Tresen, an dem man ein schnelles Frühstück oder ein leichtes Abendessen zu sich nehmen kann. Gleitende und lichtdurchlässige Paneele, teilweise aus Kunstharz, machen dieses Loft sehr dynamisch. Im offenen Zustand lassen sie das zweite Wohnzimmer frei, so dass der gesamte Raum größer wirkt. Wenn sie geschlossen sind, entsteht ein einladendes und zurückgezogenes Gästezimmer. Das Hauptziel bei diesem Umbau war es, so viel Tageslicht wie möglich in alle Räume zu lassen. Deshalb wurden in den oberen Bereichen der Innenwände waagerechte Kippfenster eingelassen, die auch für eine gute Belüftung sorgen.

]
e distribution of the loft joins the living room and dining room into a single space.
 distribution de ce loft permet de réunir les zones de jour, salon et salle à manger, en un seul espace.
diesem Loft befinden sich die tagsüber bewohnten Zonen, also das Wohnzimmer und das Esszimmer, in einem einzigen Raum.

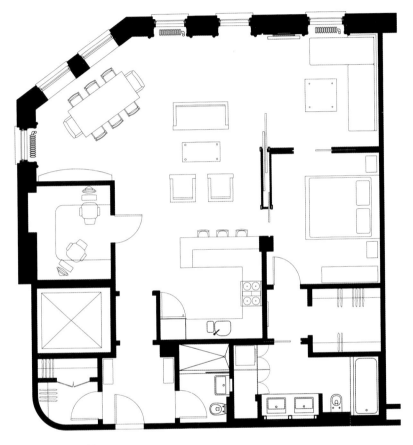

Plan Plan Grundriss

The colorful décor and the mobile windows and panels give the interior of this comfortable, elegant loft a dynamic edge.

L'agencement coloriste et les panneaux amovibles dynamisent l'intérieur de ce loft à la fois confortable et élégant.

Die farbenprächtige Dekoration und die beweglichen Paneele lassen dieses komfortable und elegante Loft dynamisch wirken.

The combination of materials and textures and shades of blue and gray create a serene ambience in the bathroom.

Dans la salle de bains, le mélange de matériaux et de textures, ainsi que les tonalités grises et bleues, créent une atmosphère de sérénité.

Im Bad entstand durch die Kombination der Materialien und Texturen und durch die Grau- und Blautöne eine gelassene Atmosphäre.

☐ Loft in Melbourne
Loft à Melbourne
Loft in Melbourne

Six Degrees Architects

This nearly square-shaped loft was reorganized to house the essential functional areas such as the bedroom, bathrooms, kitchen, and living room. The versatile space allowed for multiple possibilities but also required a carefully planned design to achieve freedom of movement, an outstanding feature of the loft. A single, gray structure serves as a wall, separating the bedroom from the kitchen area and preserving privacy in areas such as the bathroom, without the existence of a door. The floor plan incorporates a kitchen that opens onto the living room and dining area. Distinctive types of flooring visually separate each space, such as polished cement in the living room and bedroom, a parquet platform in the kitchen, and mosaic tiles in the bathroom. The décor is austere but by no means cold, and the combination of shades of gray with the luminosity of the white walls enhances the character of this loft.

Ce loft, qui suit un plan presque carré, devait être redistribué pour créer les principaux espaces de vie : chambre à coucher, salle de bains, une cuisine et un séjour salle à manger. La polyvalence de l'espace offre de multiples possibilités, mais implique un design sur mesure et bien pensé, à l'instar de ce grand mur gris qui sert de mur séparateur entre la cuisine et la chambre à coucher. Son emplacement permet à des espaces, comme la salle de bains, de bénéficier d'une intimité en dépit de l'absence de porte. Cette distribution originale s'agrémente d'une cuisine ouverte sur le séjour salle à manger. La séparation optique de chaque espace se fait par le biais de divers revêtements de sol : ciment poli au salon et dans la chambre à coucher, parquet dans la cuisine et carreaux de mosaïque dans la salle de bains. La décoration reste sobre mais jamais froide et les tons gris, contrastant avec les murs blancs et la luminosité du loft, donnent du caractère à cet espace.

Dieses Loft mit einem fast quadratischen Grundriss musste neu aufgeteilt werden, um den wichtigsten Bereichen - Schlafzimmer, Bad, Küche und kombinierten Wohn- und Esszimmer - einen Platz zuzuweisen. Die Vielseitigkeit des Raumes bot mehrere Möglichkeiten, jedoch war es wichtig, sehr genau und überlegt zu planen. Ein großes graues Möbelstück hat die Funktion einer einzigen Wand, die das Schlafzimmer von der Küche trennt. Durch dieses Möbel konnte man in bestimmten Bereichen wie dem Badezimmer Privatsphäre schaffen, ohne dass dazu eine Tür nötig war. Die originale Raumaufteilung wird durch die Küche fortgesetzt, die sich zum Wohn- und Esszimmer hin öffnet. Die verschiedenen Bodenbeläge dienen als visuelle Raumteiler für jeden Bereich: polierter Beton im Wohnzimmer und im Schlafzimmer, Parkett in der Küche und Mosaikfliesen im Bad. Die Dekoration ist schlicht, aber keinesfalls kalt, und die Grautöne bilden einen Kontrast zu den weißen Wänden und der Helligkeit im Loft. So entstand ein Raum mit viel Charakter.

The décor is austere but by no means cold, and the combination of shades of gray with the luminosity of the white walls enhances the character of this loft.
La décoration est sobre, sans être froide. Les tons gris sont élégants et contrastent avec les murs blancs et la luminosité du loft.
Die Dekoration ist schlicht, jedoch nicht kalt. Die verschiedenen Grautöne wirken sehr elegant und bilden einen Kontrast zu den weißen Wänden und dem Tageslicht.

stinctive types of flooring visually separate each space—a parquet platform in the kitchen and mosaic tiles in the bathroom.

s revêtements différents, le parquet du couloir et le grès de la salle de bains, créent une délimitation optique des espaces.

r Boden im Flur ist mit Parkett belegt und der im Badezimmer mit Fliesen, so dass die verschiedenen Bodenbeläge visuell die Räume begrenzen.

☐ Loft in Caldes de Montbui
Loft à Caldes de Montbui
Loft in Caldes de Montbui

Manel Torres / In Disseny

Although this diaphanous yet small space has no real partitions, the project design allows for it to be divided into two areas: the entrance hall, which leads to the kitchen, and the living room, which is separated from the dining room by a bookcase. The only dividers are the small false walls, such as the one that separates the dining room from the kitchen, and the sliding door of the bedroom. The bedroom is situated next to the living room and although the en suite bathroom has no door, it is well concealed within the space. The modern furniture and its careful placement result in an attractive and dynamic loft with plenty of character, thanks to the creative use of color. All sides of this apartment face the exterior, and it is surrounded by a balcony, which magnifies the feeling of space by flooding the apartment with light.

Malgré l'absence apparente de division, la conception du projet permet de définir l'espace en deux zones : le vestibule, menant à la cuisine et le salon, séparé visuellement de la salle à manger par une bibliothèque. Le faux mur qui sépare la salle à manger de la cuisine et la porte coulissante de la chambre à coucher constituent les uniques éléments séparateurs. La salle de bains est contiguë à cette pièce, protégée des regards malgré l'absence de portes. Le mobilier moderne et sa distribution bien étudiée, conjugué à l'emploi judicieux des couleurs, parachèvent un loft dynamique et attrayant doté de caractère. Le balcon qui s'enroule autour de la majeure partie du périmètre de l'appartement, a permis de pratiquer des ouvertures dans toutes les parois, laissant ainsi entrer une lumière abondante qui inonde l'intérieur et exalte la sensation d'espace.

Obwohl es in diesem Raum keine Raumteiler gibt, ist er doch so gestaltet, dass er in zwei Bereiche unterteilt zu sein scheint, nämlich in den Eingangsbereich, durch den man in die Küche gelangt, und in das Wohnzimmer, das visuell durch ein Bücherregal vom Esszimmer getrennt ist. Die einzigen Raumteiler sind die zweite Wand, die das Esszimmer von der Küche trennt, und die Schiebetür am Schlafzimmer. Neben dem Schlafzimmer liegt das Bad, das, obwohl es keine Tür besitzt, gut verborgen ist. Durch die modernen Möbel, die gelungene Aufteilung und die kreative Verwendung der Farben entstand ein dynamisches und anziehendes Loft mit sehr viel Charakter. Der Balkon, der den größten Teil der Wohnung umgibt, machte es möglich, viele Fenster einzubauen, so dass reichlich Licht ins Innere fällt und das Gefühl von Weite verstärkt wird.

The kitchen counter contains a small but clever sliding table, which increases the overall area of the work surface.

Le plan de travail de la cuisine est doté d'une petite table coulissante intégrée qui permet d'en agrandir la superficie.

In der Arbeitsfläche der Küche befindet sich ein kleiner gleitender Tisch, durch den man die Nutzfläche vergrößern kann.

materials used in the bathroom create an elegant and serene space.

matériaux utilisés dans la salle de bains configurent un espace élégant et serein.

im Bad verwendeten Materialien lassen eine elegante und schlichte Umgebung entstehen.

☐ Loft L

Ruhl Walker Architects

This rectangular loft was subdivided into different functional areas by using varied materials, changes in level, and mobile translucent partitions. The glass wall, which cuts across the loft diagonally to separate the living area from the master bedroom, is a notable feature. The master bedroom sits on a wooden platform, creating a cozy ambience of warmth and comfort, whereas the rest of the floors are polished cement. The private space behind the glass wall is made up of a bedroom and bathroom. A small desk is situated between the day and night zones, joining both areas. In the spacious lounge, a curved wall with fitted shelving stands out, accentuating the depth of the space. The elegantly wood-paneled kitchen integrates smoothly with the living area and adds a warm touch to the loft's décor.

Ce loft est un volume rectangulaire subdivisé en diverses zones grâce à l'emploi de divers matériaux, différences de niveaux et cloisons translucides amovibles. Un des points de mire est un mur de cristal qui traverse pratiquement tout le loft en diagonale et sépare la zone de séjour de la chambre à coucher principale. Cette chambre dispose d'un parquet qui lui confère confort et chaleur alors que le reste de la demeure est recouvert de ciment poli. Entre la zone de jour et de nuit, il y a un petit secrétaire qui s'intègre aux deux espaces. De même, on remarque dans le vaste séjour un mur tout en courbe qui accueille un meuble encastré, accentuant ainsi la profondeur de l'espace. La cuisine, équipée de meubles en bois très élégants, s'intègre à merveille au salon et confère une touche chaude au décor du loft.

Das Loft hat einen rechteckigen Grundriss, der durch die Verwendung unterschiedlicher Materialien, Höhenunterschiede und lichtdurchlässige, bewegliche Raumteiler in verschiedene Bereiche unterteilt wird. Ein besonders auffallendes Element ist eine Glaswand, die fast das ganze Loft diagonal durchquert und das Wohnzimmer vom Schlafzimmer trennt. Die Fußböden sind aus poliertem Beton, unter Ausnahme des Schlafzimmers, das sich auf einem Holzpodium befindet und so wärmer und komfortabler ist. Zwischen dem tagsüber und dem in der Nacht benutzten Bereich steht ein kleiner Schreibtisch, der zu beiden Räumen gehört. Im großen Wohnzimmer steht eine auffällige, gekrümmte Wand mit einem Einbaumöbel, das die Tiefe des Raums noch unterstreicht. Die Küche ist mit eleganten Holzmöbeln ausgestattet und fügt sich so perfekt in das Wohnzimmer ein. Sie verleiht dem Loft etwas mehr Wärme.

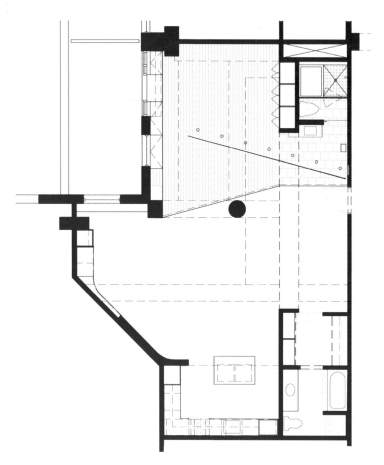

Plan Plan Grundriss

A small desk is situated between the day and night zones, joning both areas.

Entre la zone de jour et de nuit, il y a un petit secrétaire à cheval sur les deux espaces.

Zwischen den tagsüber und den nachts genutzten Bereichen wurde ein kleiner Schreibtisch aufgestellt, der von beiden Seiten zugänglich ist.

]
e glass wall, which cuts across the loft diagonally to separate the living area from the master bedroom, is a notable feature.

mur de verre traverse pratiquement tout le loft en diagonal et sépare la zone de séjour de la chambre à coucher principale.

e Glaswand durchquert das Loft diagonal und trennt den Wohnbereich vom Schlafzimmer.

☐ Loft Noho

Slade Architecture

This attractive New York loft was designed for a young photographer couple. In addition to the essential elements of any apartment, the space needed to accommodate a light table and a sizable filing cabinet. The existing space featured high ceilings and columns, which gave the loft personality; however, the available light was limited because all the windows were situated on the same wall. To overcome this problem, medium-height furniture and translucent panels were incorporated to illuminate the apartment as much as possible. The elegantly furnished kitchen is situated along one of the walls, thus opening up the space. Simple translucent fiber panels divide the day areas from the bedroom and permit the flow of natural light, while interior fluorescent lights illuminate the bookcase.

Ce beau loft new-yorkais est conçu par un jeune couple, tous deux photographes de profession. En plus des éléments d'habitat essentiels, il fallait créer un espace pour installer la table lumineuse et un grand classeur. L'espace existant disposait de hauts plafonds et de colonnes, éléments propres à la définition du style loft. En outre, l'éclairage intérieur par la lumière naturelle était réduit puisque toutes les fenêtres se trouvaient sur une seule façade. Pour résoudre se problème, l'espace a été agencé avec des meubles peu élevés et des panneaux translucides pour inonder de lumière naturelle un maximum de zones. La cuisine, au mobilier tout en élégance, est adossée à un mur très long, s'ouvrant ainsi au reste de l'espace. La séparation entre les zones de jour et de nuit se fait par le biais de panneaux translucides en fibres filtrant la lumière naturelle et illuminant la bibliothèque de lumières intérieures fluorescentes.

Dieses schöne Loft in New York wurde für ein junges Paar entworfen, beide von Beruf Fotografen. Außer den grundlegenden Elementen der Wohnung benötigte man noch Platz, um einen beleuchteten Tisch und einen großen Aktenschrank aufzustellen. Der Raum hatte schon vor dem Umbau hohe Decken und Säulen, Elemente, die seinen Charakter definieren. Allerdings fiel wenig Tageslicht ins Innere, da sich alle Fenster auf der selben Seite befinden. Um dieses Problem zu lösen, wurden halbhohe Wände und lichtdurchlässige Paneele eingezogen, so dass das Tageslicht jeden Winkel erreicht. Die elegant möblierte Küche liegt längs an einer Wand und öffnet sich zum Zentrum. Um die Wohnräume vom Schlafzimmer abzutrennen, benutzte man einfache lichtdurchlässige Paneele aus Fasern, die das Tageslicht filtern und gleichzeitig eine Leuchtstoffröhrenbeleuchtung für das Bücherregal enthalten.

Plan Plan Grundriss

The existing space featured high ceilings and columns, which gave the loft personality.
Les hauts plafonds et les colonnes, deux éléments originaux de ce loft, affichent la personnalité de cette habitation.
Die hohen Decken und die Säule, Originalelemente dieses Lofts, verleihen der Wohnung Charakter.

The minimalist and intimate bathroom is fitted out with a sink, side panels, and lamp made from resin.

La salle de bains de la chambre à coucher, à l'esthétique minimaliste, accueille un lavabo en résine, matière identique à celle des panneaux latéraux et de la lampe.

Im Bad brachte man ein Handwaschbecken aus Kunstharz an. Das gleiche Material wurde auch für die seitlichen Paneele und für die Lampe verwendet.

☐ Loft Louise

Jean Leclercq/Delices Architectes

This former office was rehabilitated so that it could be converted into dwelling space. The open spaces that characterized it have been maintained, as has the expansive rectangular floor, which is one of the attractions of this apartment. The only enclosed space is the dynamic bedroom area, which is surrounded by glass walls that can be either transparent or opaque, depending on the circumstances. The lounge boasts a fireplace which adds warmth and coziness to this elegant loft. Another important element of the décor that has been carefully studied is light, sources of which range from a small corner lamp to the large windows that maximize the flow of natural light. Most of the flooring is stained wengue wood; however, the kitchen and bathroom floors are steel or ceramic tiling in anthracite shades, materials that add character to an austere interior.

Cet ancien bureau a été restauré pour se transformer en surface habitable. Les espaces ouverts et le plan rectangulaire spacieux qui ont été conservés, définissent ce loft et en sont les caractéristiques intéressantes. L'unique pièce fermée est la chambre à coucher, délimitée par les parois de verre dont la transparence est modulable en fonction des circonstances. La cheminée du salon confère à cet élégant loft une sensation de chaleur et d'intimité. L'éclairage, fruit d'une étude extrêmement minutieuse, est un autre détail essentiel de la décoration. Il se décline dans une gamme allant d'une petite lampe de coin aux grandes fenêtres qui maximalisent l'entrée de la lumière naturelle. Le sol est en grande partie constitué de bois de wengué teinté. Toutefois, les sols de la cuisine et des salles de bains sont en acier ou carrelés dans les tons anthracite, ces matériaux donnent du caractère à un intérieur sombre.

Dieses ehemalige Büro wurde zu einer Wohnung umgebaut. Die offenen Räume behielt man ebenso wie den interessanten rechteckigen Grundriss bei. Der einzige geschlossene Raum ist das Schlafzimmer, das von Glaswänden begrenzt wird. Die Transparenz dieser Glaswände kann auf Wunsch verändert werden. Der schöne Kamin lässt das Wohnzimmer freundlich und einladend wirken. Ein anderes wichtiges Dekorationselement, das sehr sorgfältig geplant wurde, ist die Beleuchtung, die sowohl das Licht, das durch die großen Fenster fällt, umfasst, als auch die kleine Lampe in der Ecke. Der größte Teil des Bodens ist mit gefärbtem Wenge-Holz belegt, der Küchen- und der Badezimmerboden jedoch sind aus Stahl oder Keramikkacheln in Anthrazittönen. Diese Materialien lassen die Räume schlicht und edel wirken.

Light sources range from a small corner lamp to large windows that maximize the flow of natural light.

L'éclairage est le fruit d'une étude extrêmement minutieuse : depuis la petite lampe d'angle jusqu'aux baies vitrées qui permettent à la lumière naturelle d'entrer à flot.

Die Beleuchtung wurde sehr sorgfältig behandelt, von der kleinen Ecklampe bis zu den Fenstern, durch die reichlich Tageslicht einfällt.

The kitchen features steel and ceramic in anthracitic shades that add character to an austere interior.

Dans la cuisine, les revêtements comme l'acier et la céramique déclinés dans des tons anthracite, donnent du caractère à un intérieur sombre.

Die Küche ist mit Stahl und anthrazitfarbener Keramik verkleidet. Diese Materialien wirken schlicht und elegant.

bathroom combines gray mosaic tiling with a white sink and bath, an elegant and timeless combination.

s la salle de bains, les carrelages gris contrastent avec le lavabo et la baignoire immaculés, mariant l'élégance à l'intemporalité.

3ad bilden die grauen Kacheln einen Kontrast zu dem weißen Waschbecken und der Badewanne, eine elegante und zeitlose Kombination.

☐ **Loft Annalisa**

Studio Del Portico

The refurbishment of this loft involved converting two different apartments into a single home. The preexisting structure lacked any aesthetic or architectural value, so the idea was to strip it away, leaving the brick wall and arched vaults exposed to allow in more light and endow the space with greater expansiveness and personality. As a result of the conversion, the bedrooms were situated on the upper level, acheeving greater intimacy. The daytime area became a single space comprising taking in the living room, the modern kitchen, and the bathroom. The decoration plays a significant role, as it adds character while avoiding the industrial austerity and minimalism typical of many lofts. Similarly, the lighting creates a warm atmosphere, while some of the accessories, such as the bathroom mirror, reveal the distinctive taste of the owner.

La restauration de ce loft a permis de transformer deux appartements différents en une habitation unique. L'ancienne structure manquait de caractère esthétique et architectural. Le but était de garder la clarté, un mur apparent et un arc de voûte pour agrandir l'espace et lui donner du caractère. La nouvelle distribution situe la zone de nuit à l'étage supérieur pour préserver ainsi l'intimité, tandis que la zone de jour est devenue un espace unique abritant la salle de séjour, la cuisine moderne et la salle de bains. La décoration joue un rôle significatif puisqu'elle marque la personnalité de l'habitation, fuyant le minimalisme et l'austérité propres à l'esthétique industrielle des autres lofts. De même, l'éclairage dispense une ambiance chaleureuse et certains éléments de la maison, à l'instar du miroir original de la salle de bains, affichent le goût particulier de la propriétaire.

Beim Umbau dieses Lofts machte man aus zwei Wohnungen eine. Die vorhandene Struktur war weder ästhetisch noch architektonisch schön oder interessant. Allerdings sollte eine unverputzte Wand und der Bogen des Gewölbes erhalten bleiben, und viel Licht sollte in die Räume fallen, um der Wohnung Weite und Persönlichkeit zu geben. Nach der neuen Aufteilung liegen nun die Schlafzimmer in der oberen Etage, wo es mehr Privatsphäre gibt. Die Räume, in denen man sich tagsüber aufhält, also das Wohnzimmer, die moderne Küche und das Bad, bilden eine räumliche Einheit. Die Innengestaltung ist sehr wichtig in dieser Wohnung, sie ist persönlich und vermeidet die Schlichtheit und den Minimalismus, der für die industrielle Ästhetik anderer Loftwohnungen typisch ist. Auch die Beleuchtung lässt eine warme Atmosphäre entstehen, und einige Elemente des Hauses wie der originelle Spiegel im Bad zeigen den einzigartigen Geschmack der Eigentümerin.

e decoration plays a significant role, as it adds character while avoiding the industrial austerity and minimalism typical of many lofts.

ménagement intérieur joue un rôle significatif, car il fuit l'austérité et le minimalisme propres à l'esthétique industrielle des autres lofts.

e Dekoration spielt eine entscheidende Rolle. Die große Schlichte und der Minimalismus, der typisch für die industrielle Ästhetik anderer Lofts sind, werden vermieden.

daytime area became a single space taking in the living room and the modern kitchen from stainless steel.

zone de jour s'est métamorphosée en un seul espace qui unit la salle à manger et la cuisine moderne en acier inoxydable.

gibt nur einen einzigen Raum für den Tag, in dem sich das Wohnzimmer und die moderne Küche aus Edelstahl vereinen.

☐ N House
Maison N
N Haus

Studio Damilano

This elegant two-bedroom loft is divided into individual areas by means of panels and partitions that create unique and versatile spaces. A glass wall separates the dining area from the living room, resulting in a framed effect that is apparent from both sides. The use of white and pure lines adds serenity and luminosity to the ambience. Another panel of wooden sheets divides the dining area from the loft's entrance, and a third partition similarly separates the kitchen from the rest of the apartment. Transparency and light are fundamental to the interior design, evident in the white walls and sofas that bring the kitchen to life. Dark wood has been used for contrast, adding a note of distinction. In the bathroom, the glass walls of the shower also set off the elevated bathing area. The absence of superfluous elements allows serenity and tranquility to emanate from this loft.

Ce loft de deux pièces, tout en élégance, est divisé par des panneaux définissant des espaces originaux et changeants. Une immense fenêtre intérieure sépare la salle à manger du salon et encadre le paysage intérieur sur deux côtés. Les lignes blanches, presque pures, définissent une atmosphère de sérénité, tout en luminosité. Un autre mur lambrissé sépare la salle à manger de l'entrée du loft. Une troisième cloison sépare la cuisine du reste de l'habitation. La transparence et la légèreté sont les notes qui dominent l'aménagement. Le blanc des murs et des divans se retrouve également dans la cuisine. Le bois sombre sert de contrepoint et apporte une note d'élégance. Dans la salle de bains, la paroi de la douche sert également de cloison pour séparer la baignoire, située sur un niveau supérieur. La sobriété est un autre des points caractérisant ce loft qui, grâce à l'absence d'élément superflu, dégage une ambiance de sérénité.

Diese elegante Zweizimmerwohnung ist mit Paneelen unterteilt, die originelle und sich ändernde Räume schaffen. Ein riesiges Fenster trennt das Speisezimmer vom Wohnzimmer und umrahmt die häusliche Landschaft, die man von beiden Seiten aus sieht. Die weißen, fast reinen Linien lassen die Wohnung ruhig und hell wirken. Ein weiteres Paneel aus Holzplatten trennt das Speisezimmer vom Eingangsbereich. Ein dritter Raumteiler trennt die Küche vom übrigen Raum. Transparenz und Leichtigkeit sind die vorherrschenden Merkmale der Gestaltung dieser Räume. Die weißen Wände und die Sofas sind auch in der Küche präsent. Als Kontrast wurde dunkles Holz benutzt, das die Wohnung sehr edel wirken lässt. Im Bad dient die Glastür der Dusche auch zum Abtrennen der Badewanne, die sich auf einer höheren Ebene befindet. Ein anderer auffallender Charakterzug dieses Lofts ist seine Schlichtheit. Es gibt keine überflüssigen Elemente, die die ruhige Wohnumgebung unterbrechen.

Plan Plan Grundriss

Dark wood has been used to contrast with the white walls and sofas, adding a note of distinction.

Le bois sombre s'offre en contrepoint aux murs et au divan blanc et apporte une touche d'élégance.

Das dunkle Holz bildet einen Kontrast zu den Wänden und dem weißen Sofa und lässt alles noch edler wirken.

The glass walls of the shower also set off the elevated bathing area.

Les parois de verre de la douche définissent à leur tour la zone de la salle de bains, située sur un niveau supérieur.

Die Glaswände der Dusche definieren gleichzeitig den Badezimmerbereich, der sich auf einer höheren Ebene befindet.

Steve House
Maison Steve
Steve Haus

Marco Guido Savorelli

The aim of this far-reaching refurbishment was to bring together all the functions of a home in a single, albeit fragmented living space. To achieve this, partitions were knocked down and the structure was emphasized to turn it into a skeleton that articulates the three main living areas in the house. The doors were substituted by floor-to-ceiling mobile panels that fit perfectly into the walls when they are closed. The lacquered rosewood furniture was custom-made and its precise, elegant geometric lines play a key role in the project. The central space is occupied by the dining room and kitchen, subtly incorporated behind a half-height partition, while the bedroom is dominated by the marble bathtub that doubles as a headboard for the bed. The third area is a flexible space designed for working and meditating, with a practical stool and table integrated into the wall.

Cette restauration profonde s'inscrit dans un projet visant à réunir toutes les fonctions en un espace habitable unique mais fragmenté entraînant la démolition des cloisons et la modification de la structure. Celle-ci s'est métamorphosée en une ossature qui distribue les trois espaces principaux de l'habitation. Les portes sont remplacées par des panneaux amovibles, allant du sol au plafond. Une fois fermés, ils s'encastrent parfaitement dans les murs. Les meubles en palissandre laqué affichent un design unique et deviennent, grâce à leurs lignes géométriques précises et élégantes, partie intégrante du projet. Le salon salle à manger et la cuisine –subtilement intégrée derrière une cloison à mi-hauteur – occupent l'espace central. Dans la chambre à coucher, la baignoire en marbre qui sert de tête de lit s'inscrit en point de mire. Le troisième univers est défini par une pièce polyvalente servant de lieu de travail ou de méditation, dotée d'un tabouret et d'une table pliante intégrés au mobilier mural.

Das Ziel bei diesem Totalumbau war es, alle Wohnfunktionen in einem einzigen, bewohnbaren, aber unterteilten Raum unterzubringen. Dazu wurden die Trennwände abgerissen und die Struktur hervorgehoben, die zum Skelett wurde, von dem die drei wichtigsten Wohnbereiche ausgehen. Die Türen wurden durch bewegliche Paneele ersetzt, die vom Boden bis zur Decke reichen und die sich im geschlossenen Zustand perfekt in die Wände einfügen. Die Möbel aus lackiertem Palisander wurden von den Eigentümern selbst entworfen und bilden ein grundlegendes Element des Gesamtbildes mit seinen präzisen und eleganten geometrischen Linien. Das kombinierte Wohn- und Esszimmer, das nur leicht durch eine halbhohe Wand abgetrennt ist, befindet sich im Zentrum. Im Schlafzimmer steht eine auffallende Badewanne aus Marmor, die gleichzeitig das Kopfteil des Bettes bildet. Der dritte Wohnbereich ist ein angenehmer Raum zum Arbeiten und Meditieren, in dem ein Schemel und Klapptisch stehen, die in die Wandmöbel integriert sind.

eeping with the philosophy of feng shui, the ultimate aim of the project is to create a balanced and harmonious home by establishing a style of contemporary lines.

spirant de la philosophie feng shui, le projet vise à créer une habitation équilibrée et harmonieuse dans un style aux lignes pures et contemporaines.

ses Loft wurde nach den Regeln des Feng Shui gestaltet, so dass eine ausgeglichene und harmonische Wohnung mit reinen und zeitgemäßen Linien entstand.

setting can be adapted to both work and meditation, with a practical stool and table integrated into the wall furnishings.

abouret et une table pliante, intégrés au mobilier mural, configurent un espace polyvalent servant de lieu de travail ou de méditation.

Hocker und ein Klapptisch, die in die Wandmöbel integriert sind, prägen den Raum, der als Arbeits- oder Meditationszimmer genutzt wird.

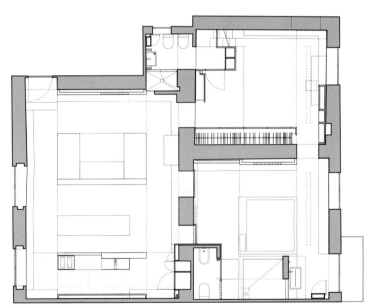

Plan Plan Grundriss

The apartment stands out on account of the purity of its design, the integration of its spaces and the subtle contrast between its finishings, furniture, and flooring.

L'appartement est caractérisé par la pureté du design, l'intégration des différents espaces et un contraste subtil entre finitions, meubles et carrelages.

Die Wohnung zeichnet sich durch ihr klares, reines und integriertes Design aus, sowie durch die leichten Kontraste zwischen den Wänden, Möbeln und Bodenbelägen.

Loft Putxet

Eduard Samsó

Upon entering this loft we feel we are being watched by a cyclopean eye hanging from the ceiling, suspended from a horizontal bar by a spring that allows it to look in every possible direction. It is as if we were in a photographer,s studio, seeing flashes of everything that happens within the house and the objects that construct and inhabit the interior. This mobile and flexible eye moves through the centre of the loft offering the spectacle of television from any point of view, while its screen reflects our faces and gives testimony of the course of domestic activities concentrated in a space that is uniform, without evident visible separations and with suggestive lines that indicate different floor levels.

En entrant dans ce loft, on se sent comme observé par un oeil de cyclope qui pend du toit, suspendu à une barre horizontale attachée à un ressort qui permet de l'actionner dans tous les sens. Comme si nous étions dans un atelier de photographe, on reçoit les flashs de tous les faits et gestes instantanés qui se déroulent dans l'habitation et de la constance des objets qui construisent et meublent l'intérieur. L'oeil mobile et flexible se promène au centre du loft, offrant le spectacle télévisé de n'importe quelle ligne de mire, tandis que notre visage se reflète sur son écran. Il témoigne du déroulement des activités domestiques, regroupées dans un espace uniforme, sans séparation physique évidente et à l'aide de lignes sinueuses qui dessinent des sols de niveaux différents.

Wenn man dieses Loft betritt, hat man das Gefühl, von einem Zyklopenauge beobachtet zu werden, das von der Decke herabhängt, an einer waagerechten Stange mit einer Feder, die es in alle Richtungen lenken kann. So als ob wir uns in einem Fotografiestudio befinden würden, erspähen wir Momentaufnahmen von allem, was in dieser Wohnung geschehen ist, und spüren die Beständigkeit der Objekte, die das Innere erschaffen und bewohnen. Das bewegliche und flexible Auge gleitet durch das Zentrum des Lofts und macht das Fernsehen von jedem Winkel aus möglich, während der Bildschirm unser Gesicht widerspiegelt und den Ablauf der häuslichen Tätigkeiten bezeugt, die sich alle in einem einzigen Raum abspielen, ohne offensichtliche physische Raumteiler. Lediglich die verschiedenen Bodenhöhen deuten die verschiedenen Bereiche an.

The mobile and flexible TV moves through the center of the loft offering a view of the television.

Un téléviseur mobile, à hauteur réglable, se promène au centre du loft et permet d'admirer le spectacle de n'importe quel angle.

Ein beweglicher, in der Höhe verstellbarer Fernseher gleitet durch das Zentrum des Lofts, so dass man von überall aus fernsehen kann.

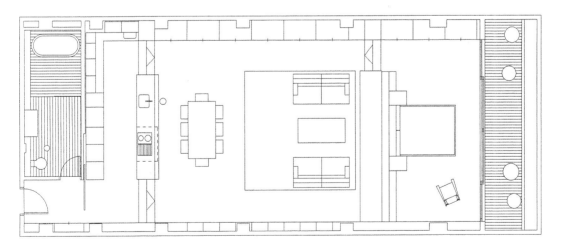

Plan Plan Grundriss

The contours of the extractor break up the kitchen and the dining room with its solid posture of quiet, balance, and stability.

Les contours de la hotte aspirante qui séparent la cuisine de la salle à manger, affichent calme, stabilité et équilibre.

Der Umriss der Dunstabzugshaube trennt die Küche vom Speisezimmer und vermittelt Ruhe, Stabilität und Gleichgewicht.

☐ Waxter Apartment
Appartement Waxter
Waxter Apartment

Slade Architecture

This small space, besides providing the comfort of a home, was also designed to exhibit works of art. The owner, an avid art dealer, looked to transform his apartment into a space that integrated both his domestic and working environment and provided the stability, comfort and utility needed for a fast-paced and stressful lifestyle. Within the small floor plan, infinite lines are drawn that extend over the uniform plane, eliminating limits and painting a gust of fog to erase the traces of any volumes that may be visible. A decision was made to establish flexible areas to group the basic bedrooms within the small space on the single level. A simple and elegant space is found on the second level, for the use of guests, business people, and works of art that complement the silence of this setting.

Cet espace réduit vise à reproduire le bien-être d'une habitation tout en permettant d'exposer des œuvres d'art. Le propriétaire, passionné d'achat et vente d'objets d'art, souhaite convertir cet appartement en un habitat unissant l'environnement domestique à l'univers professionnel. Lieu de vie qui doit être à la fois stable, commode et fonctionnel pour contrebalancer un style de vie vertigineux marqué par le stress. Des lignes infinies, partant d'un volume compact, s'ouvrent sur un plan uniforme. Effaçant les limites, elles esquissent une nuée cotonneuse à l'instar d'un brouillard, où l'on devine la présence des corps désireux de se manifester. La création de nombreuses zones flexibles permet d'intégrer les pièces essentielles au sein d'un espace unique de petites dimensions. Un espace simple et élégant, en retrait, dans l'attente des invités, des marchands et des œuvres d'art qui meublent le silence exprimé par la toile de fond.

Dieser kleine Raum sollte nicht nur zu einer Wohnung zum Wohlfühlen werden, sondern er sollte auch als Ausstellungssaal für Kunstwerke dienen. Der Eigentümer widmet sich dem An- und Verkauf von Kunst und er wollte diesen Raum zu einer Umgebung machen, in der sich das Wohnen mit seiner beruflichen Welt mischt und der so bequem, beständig und zweckmäßig ist, und als Ruhepunkt in seinem vom Stress gezeichneten Leben dient. Von einem kompakten Grundriss ausgehend wurden unendliche Linien gezogen, die diesen einheitlichen Grundriss fortsetzen und Begrenzungen ausradieren. Hier kann man die Präsenz aller Körper aufhängen, die sichtbar sein sollen. Um die wichtigsten Räume auf einer so kleinen Fläche anzuordnen, wurden sehr flexible Zonen angelegt. Ein einfacher und eleganter Raum befindet sich im Hintergrund und wartet auf Gäste, Kunsthändler und Kunstwerke, die die Stille, die in diesem Bereich herrscht, noch kompletter machen.

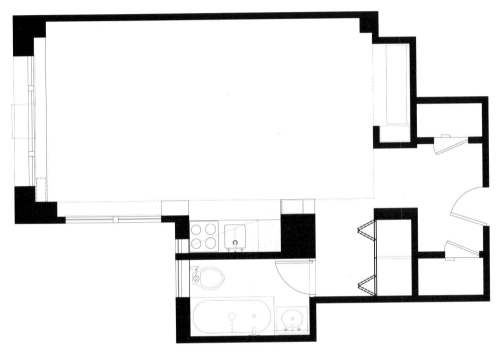

Plan Plan Grundriss

The different functions are enclosed by a single multifunctional veil, that converts the whole interior into an enormous, disconcerting insinuation.

Les différentes fonctions sont disposées sous un seul voile multifonctionnel, laissant deviner l'intérieur de manière surprenante.

Die verschiedenen Funktionen sind unter einem einzigen multifunktionellen Schleier verborgen, der den Raum auf interessante Weise verwandelt.

A decision was made to establish flexible areas to group the basic bedrooms within the small space on the single level.

La création de nombreuses zones flexibles permet d'intégrer les pièces essentielles au sein d'un espace unique de petites dimensions.

Um die wichtigsten Räume auf so kleiner Fläche anzuordnen, wurden sehr flexible und weite Bereiche angelegt.

An atmosphere of stability, comfort, and utility was created for a fast-paced, stress-filled lifestyle.

En contrepoint au rythme vertigineux du style de vie, l'atmosphère créée communique sérénité, stabilité et confort.

Um der rasenden Hektik des modernen Lebens etwas entgegenzusetzen, schuf man eine ruhige, gelassene, beständige und komfortable Wohnung.

☐ Loft Frankie

Joan Bach

This small, fresh loft is a fine example of how a functional and attractive apartment can be achieved through the optimal organization of space. The bedroom has been situated on a mezzanine, taking full advantage of the building's high ceilings. The study, which receives abundant natural light, is located below the bedroom and contains a small table and a unique lamp. The living room includes a sofa bed and a small pouf, which serves as a coffee table. The kitchen is situated behind one of the few walls in the loft and is connected to the rest of the space by means of an opening that also serves as a small bar. The wooden floors and the free flow of natural light through the large windows lend the apartment a certain warmth. The careful design of the space and the furniture selected make this small loft feel anything but chaotic or cramped.

Ce petit loft innovateur est un exemple parfait de réalisation d'un appartement fonctionnel et attrayant grâce à une organisation judicieuse de l'espace. La chambre à coucher est située sur un entresol, utilisant au maximum les hauts plafonds de l'édifice. Le bureau, inondé de lumière naturelle, est situé sous la chambre à coucher. Il dispose d'une table et d'une lampe. L'agencement du salon décline un canapé convertible et un petit pouf servant de petite table à café. La cuisine, lovée derrière un des rares murs du loft, est reliée au reste de l'espace par le biais d'une ouverture servant également de petit bar. Les parquets et la lumière naturelle, qui pénètre sans entrave par les grandes baies vitrées, dotent l'appartement d'une certaine chaleur. Le design minutieux de l'espace et le mobilier sélectionné inscrivent ce loft dans une perception qui n'a rien de chaotique ou d'étriquée.

Dieses kleine und innovative Loft ist ein gutes Beispiel dafür, wie man durch eine gute Organisation des Raumes eine funktionelle und moderne Wohnung einrichten kann. Das Schlafzimmer liegt auf einem Zwischengeschoss, so nutzte man die hohen Decken des Gebäudes maximal aus. Das Arbeitszimmer, in das viel Tageslicht fällt, liegt unter dem Schlafzimmer und ist mit einem Tisch und einer Lampe ausgestattet. Im Wohnzimmer stehen ein Bettsofa und ein kleiner Sitzwürfel, der auch als Kaffeetischchen dient. Hinter einer der wenigen Wände des Lofts verbirgt sich die Küche, die mit dem übrigen Raum durch eine Öffnung verbunden ist, die auch als kleiner Tresen dient. Die Böden aus Holz und das Licht, das überall durch die großen Fenster fällt, lassen die Wohnung sehr freundlich wirken. Die sorgfältige Gestaltung des Raumes und die Auswahl der Möbel machen aus diesem kleinen Loft einen organisierten und groß wirkenden Raum.

interior space is magnified by the use of white, and the windows establish visual continuity with the rest of the loft.

olanc accentue la sensation d'espace intérieur et les fenêtres instaurent une continuité visuelle avec le reste du loft.

Farbe Weiß lässt die Räumlichkeiten sehr weit wirken, und die Fenster stellen einen visuellen Bezug zu dem übrigen Raum her.

The small kitchen is connected to the rest of the space by means of an opening that also serves as a small bar.

La cuisine, de petites dimensions, s'intègre au reste de l'espace grâce à une ouverture qui fait office de bar.

Die kleine Küche ist in den übrigen Raum durch eine Öffnung integriert, die gleichzeitig als Tresen dient.

☐ Fraternitat Penthouse
Duplex Fraternitat
Fraternitat Duplex

Joan Bach

Simplicity and color are the main themes of this project: a simple, uncluttered apartment with a mezzanine, where the distribution of space is delimited by specially chosen furniture. The predominant colors are red, white, and black, giving the loft and furniture a bold note. The bedroom with en suite bathroom, the kitchen area, and a small balcony are situated on the first level. The apartment enjoys natural light, which flows in through the balcony. The day area comprises a dining room furnished with a modern white table and chairs and a unique standing lamp, an American-style kitchen, and a Chesterfield sofa that lends a classic touch and contrasts well with the loft's modern aspect. The lightweight metal staircase leading to the mezzanine is a decorative element in itself.

Sobriété et couleur sont les caractéristiques essentielles qui définissent ce projet : un appartement sobre et dépouillé, doté d'un entresol, où la distribution de l'espace se fait par un choix précis de mobilier. Le rouge, le blanc et le noir, couleurs dominantes, confèrent à l'ensemble une touche osée. Le premier étage accueille une chambre à coucher dotée d'une salle de bains intégrée, la cuisine et un petit balcon. L'appartement bénéficie de la lumière naturelle qui pénètre par le balcon. La zone de jour comprend la salle à manger aménagée, comprenant une table blanche moderne et des sièges, un seul et unique lampadaire, la cuisine américaine et un divan Chesterfield dont la touche classique tranche bien avec la modernité du loft. L'aérien escalier métallique, menant à l'entresol, est en lui-même, un élément décoratif.

Die Schlichtheit und die Farben sind die wichtigsten Aspekte bei der Planung dieser Wohnung, ein einfaches und leeres Apartment mit einem Zwischengeschoss, in dem die Raumaufteilung durch die sorgfältige Auswahl der Möbel erreicht wird. Die vorherrschenden Farben sind Rot, Weiß und Schwarz, eine sehr gewagte Farbkombination. Auf der ersten Ebene liegen ein Schlafzimmer mit Badezimmer, die Küche und ein kleiner Balkon. Durch diesen Balkon fällt Tageslicht in die Wohnung. In dem Bereich, in dem man sich vor allem am Tage aufhält, befindet sich ein Esszimmer mit einem modernen weißen Tisch und Stühlen und einer Stehlampe. Daran schließt sich eine offene Küche an und ein Chesterfield-Sofa fällt ins Auge, das der Wohnung, die ansonsten sehr modern gestaltet ist, eine klassische Note verleiht. Die leichte Metalltreppe, die in das Zwischengeschoss führt, stellt schon an sich ein dekoratives Element dar.

The apartment enjoys natural light, which flows in through the balcony and illuminates the day area.

L'appartement bénéficie d'une abondante lumière naturelle qui inonde l'intérieur par la fenêtre du balcon, illuminant ainsi la zone de jour.

Diese Wohnung ist sehr hell, denn reichlich Tageslicht dringt durch das Balkonfenster und erhellt den tagsüber bewohnten Bereich.

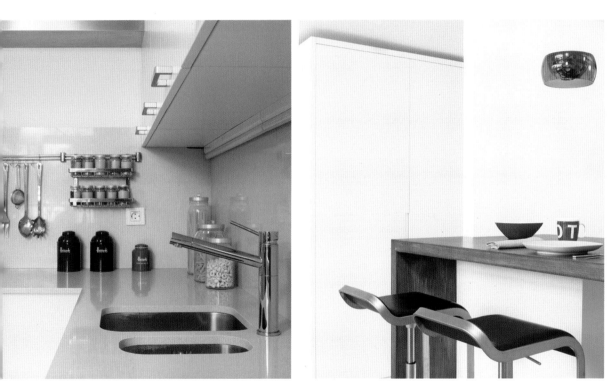

American-style kitchen is directly connected with the dining area and highlights the continuity of the whole space.

uisine américaine, qui s'intègre à la zone de la salle à manger, exalte la continuité de l'espace total.

offene Küche ist in das Esszimmer integriert und unterstreicht die Kontinuität des gesamten Raumes.

☐ Smart Apartment

Appartement Smart

Smart Apartment

Smart Design Studio

The refurbishment of this small studio in a 1920s building in the center of Sydney has turned an uncomfortable studio into a one-bedroom apartment. A sliding door designed by Tim Richardson and a work of art in itself serves to separate or join the bedroom and the living area, emphasizing the flexibility of this minimalist home. A lacquered red unit serves as a container for all the electrical appliances and closets while maintaining the unity of the apartment. It is far more than a mere series of closets, for it constitutes an original piece with a personality all its own. The original tiles in the bathroom have been preserved, along with the window frames, to achieve a greater visual impact. Despite its limited dimensions, the apartment appears spacious and bright, thanks to the sunshine and the use of simple lines in the design.

La restauration de ce petit studio - situé dans une propriété des années vingt au cœur de Sydney – a transformé un espace peu pratique en un appartement d'une seule pièce. Afin de séparer le salon de la chambre, une porte coulissante a été utilisée. Cette porte – crée par Tim Richardson – est une véritable œuvre d'art qui sert à unir les deux pièces tout en accentuant la flexibilité de cette habitation minimaliste. Un meuble laqué rouge offre un espace pour ranger les appareils électroménagers et dissimuler les armoires, tout en préservant l'unité de l'appartement. Il va sans dire que ce meuble n'est pas un simple jeu de placards mais une oeuvre originale pleine de caractère. La salle de bains a conservé ses tomettes originales et ses cadres de fenêtres pour exalter l'impact visuel. Malgré ses dimensions réduites, l'ensemble paraît ample et diaphane grâce à la lumière naturelle et au design épuré des lignes.

Durch die Renovierung dieser kleinen Studiowohnung in einem Gebäude aus den Zwanzigerjahren im Zentrum von Sydney wurde aus einem ungemütlichen Studio eine freundliche Einzimmerwohnung. Wohn- und Schlafzimmer werden durch eine von Tim Richardson gestaltete Schiebetür voneinander getrennt, die als eigenständiges Kunstobjekt fungiert. Durch diese Tür kann man das Schlafzimmer zu einem Teil des Wohnzimmers machen, und so die kleine Wohnung leicht umgestalten. Ein rot lackiertes Möbelstück dient der Unterbringung der Haushaltsgeräte und Schränke. Es trägt zur Einheitlichkeit in der ganzen Wohnung bei. Ohne Zweifel handelt es sich bei diesem Möbel nicht nur um eine einfache Zusammenstellung von Schränken, sondern um ein sehr originelles Stück. Die Originalkacheln im Bad und die Fensterrahmen ließ man, wie sie waren, um den visuellen Eindruck zu verstärken. Obwohl es sich um einen sehr kleinen Raum handelt, wirkt er durch das einfallende Tageslicht und die einfachen Linien im Ganzen weit und transparent.

A lacquered red closet conceals all the electrical appliances while maintaining the unity of the apartment.

Le grand meuble laqué rouge offre un espace pour ranger les appareils électroménagers, tout en préservant l'unité de l'appartement.

Ein rot lackiertes Möbelstück dient der Unterbringung der Haushaltsgeräte und hält die Einheitlichkeit der Wohnung bei.

original tiles in the bathroom have been preserved, along with the window frames, to achieve a greater visual impact.

céramiques de la salle de bains sont d'origine et les cadres des fenêtres conservés pour souligner l'effet optique.

Originalkacheln im Bad und die Fensterrahmen ließ man, wie sie waren, um den visuellen Eindruck zu verstärken.

Photo credits Crédits photographiques Fotonachweis